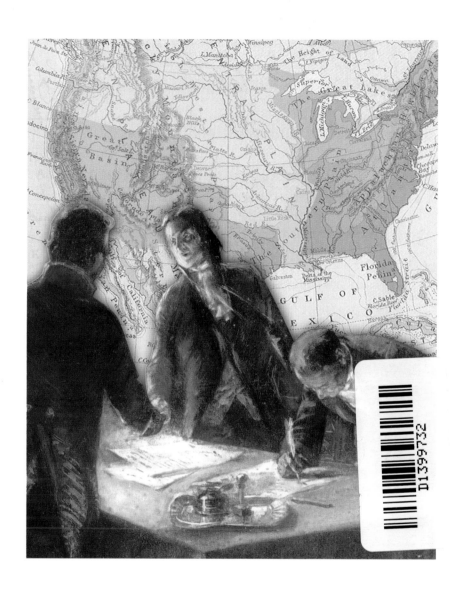

Expanding the Nation

Jill K. Mulhall, M.Ed.

Table of Contents

A Young Country Expands

The United States was not a very big place at the beginning of the 1800s. The country's 16 states were all located in one thin strip of land in the East. None of them reached past the Mississippi River. The country was made up of less than a million square miles.

By the end of the century, the United States was a world power. It controlled more than three million square miles.

▼ This map shows how the United States grew during the 1800s.

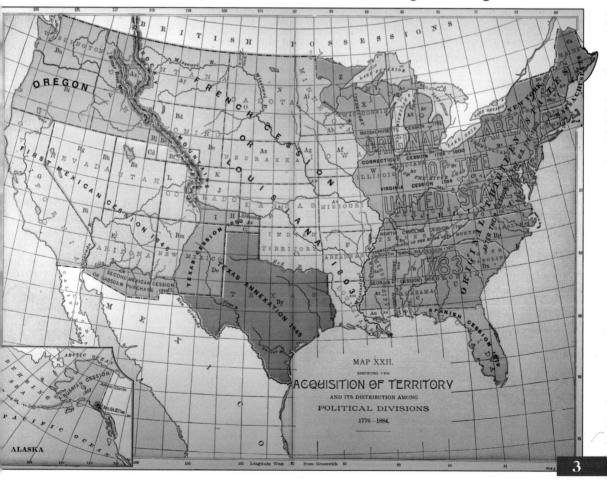

Taking New Lands

The United States began the 1800s as a small, new nation. By the beginning of the 1900s, it was very different. It stretched from the Atlantic Ocean to the Pacific Ocean.

America gained its new lands in different ways. Sometimes it bought land from other countries. Politicians and **diplomats** (DIP-luh-matz) made deals that helped America grow. Other times, the country went to war and took lands by force. These **territories** (TAIR-uh-tor-eez) came at a cost of lives, not just dollars.

Who Makes a Treaty?

A treaty is an agreement between two nations. It can end a war. It can also be an agreement to buy land. The United States president can make treaties on his own. Then, they must be approved by the Senate. The House of Representatives must also approve any treaty that involves money.

▼ The United States capitol building in 1800

The new lands brought opportunities to American **citizens** (SIT-uh-zuhnz). They found that the lands held valuable **natural resources**. So, they were able to trade with many more countries.

▼ This painting shows some of the ways the Americans moved from the East to the West.

The Land Nobody Wanted

In 1775, the colonists in America went to war with Great Britain to win their independence. But, the British were not the only ones who held land in the New World. Other European rulers also sent explorers to claim land in America.

In 1682, a group of French explorers claimed a huge area of land in the West. It started at the Gulf of Mexico and spread north. They called this territory Louisiana after their king, Louis XIV. The French did not think this land was very valuable. Only a few French settlers came to live there.

A Powerful Leader

Napoleon Bonaparte came to power in France in 1799. He was a dictator, and he did not listen to anyone else's opinion. Napoleon wanted to take over the entire world. He led his army into many wars. He was successful for years. But in the end, he pushed the French soldiers too far. By 1814, his army was defeated.

Napoleon Bonaparte

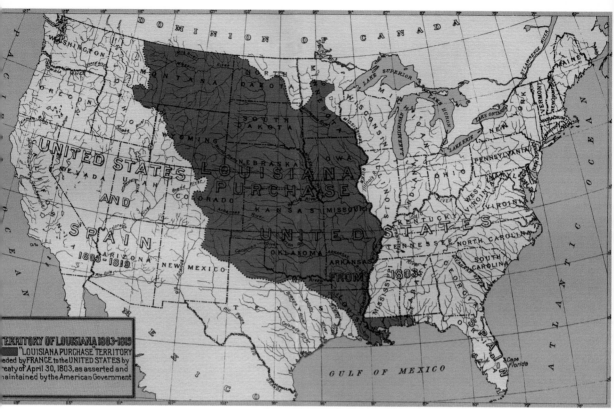

▲ This map shows how large the Louisiana Territory was.

Then, the king of France gave Louisiana to Spain for their help in a war against Great Britain. But in 1800, Spain gave it back to France. Nobody thought the land was worth anything. So they did not worry about holding on to it.

Liar, Liar

Napoleon got Spain to give Louisiana back to France. Napoleon told King Charles IV of Spain that he would create a new country in Italy. He said Charles' daughter and son-in-law could rule the new land. In return, the Spanish king gave Louisiana back to France. But Napoleon had lied. He never gave the Italian land to Spain.

Getting More Than We Bargained For

The French made many people angry when they took over Louisiana again in 1800. They told the Americans that they could not use the Mississippi River anymore. Traders had used this river to move goods to the South. The French also stopped letting Americans store their goods in the city of New Orleans.

Thomas Jefferson became the third president of the United States in 1801. He knew that Napoleon had a great army. Jefferson was worried that France would send soldiers to Louisiana.

Signing the Louisiana ▶
Purchase

Why Did He Sell?

Napoleon had many reasons for selling Louisiana. He needed money to fight his wars. He also did not want to worry about a territory so far away from France. He wanted to give all of his attention to Europe.

All Alone in France

The American diplomats had to make this big decision all by themselves. There was no way to talk to anyone in the United States. They were not sure that the president would want them to buy the whole territory. They certainly did not know what the country would think about spending 15 million dollars. They were brave to agree to the sale.

◀ The United States taking control of New Orleans

Some people in the United States started to say the country should go to war with France. They even suggested getting Great Britain to fight with them. Jefferson wanted to avoid going to war. He sent two diplomats to France to offer to buy New Orleans.

The men were surprised when they got to France. The French offered to sell not just New Orleans, but all of Louisiana!

The Americans offered eight million dollars for the territory. France said they wanted fifteen million. After some talking, the two Americans agreed. They signed the Louisiana Purchase on April 30, 1803.

Doubling the Country at a Bargain Price

Jefferson was very excited when he heard about the Louisiana Purchase treaty. He had dreamed of making America bigger. Suddenly it was twice as big!

Some people in the country were worried that the territory was too expensive. But, the House of Representatives and the Senate approved the sale.

The Spanish were angry when they heard about what had happened. They knew Napoleon had cheated them to take control of Louisiana. They accused the United States of buying stolen land. Jefferson told the Spanish leaders that this fight was between France and Spain. America would not get involved. Spain backed down. They did not want to fight powerful France.

The United States took control of Louisiana on December 20, 1803. It was an exciting day for the country.

Much More Than Louisiana

Sometimes when we think of the Louisiana Territory, we get it confused with the state of Louisiana. But the territory was much, much bigger. In fact, the land eventually made up all or part of 14 different states.

The United States had almost 828,000 square miles (about 2 million square km) of new land to explore. America had bought this land for the bargain price of about four cents an acre. Many call this the greatest real estate deal in history.

Meriwether Lewis

William Clark

The Corps of Discovery

Jefferson wanted to know all about America's new lands. So, he sent men on an **expedition** (eks-puh-DISH-uhn). They traveled across the Louisiana Territory. Then, they came home and reported on everything they saw. A man named Meriwether Lewis led the group. His friend William Clark joined him. This trip helped Americans learn about the West.

Defending the Continent

The United States was not the only country going through changes in the 1800s. Spain controlled many lands in Central and South America. People from these countries began to want their freedom. By 1821, most of them had declared their independence from Spain. Americans wanted to support these new nations. They understood how hard it was to start a new country.

On the other hand, Europeans were not supportive. There were rumors that the European countries would join together. Then, they would attack the weak, new nations. If America supported these nations, it would also be in danger.

▼ Government leaders, including James Monroe, discuss the Monroe Doctrine.

Unpopular Words

Americans were very proud of the Monroe Doctrine. But it was not very popular elsewhere. The small, new countries did not like their northern neighbor being so bossy. The European countries thought it was a silly announcement. They knew that they could overpower the United States if they wanted. This doctrine has stood the test of time. America still follows this policy today.

▼ **The Monroe Doctrine**

President James Monroe decided to make a strong statement to the world. On December 2, 1823, he asked Congress to approve a new policy. This policy was called the Monroe **Doctrine**.

The Monroe Doctrine had two main points. First it said the nations in the Americas were "free and independent." This meant that they should be respected by the European nations. The second point was that no foreign countries could set up new colonies in the Americas.

The United States was still a young country. And yet, its president was telling the world that Americans could protect themselves and their neighbors.

Americans Move into Texas

General Antonio Lopez de Santa Anna

Mexico gained its independence from Spain in 1821. This huge country was even bigger than the United States at that time.

The Mexican government decided to let Americans move into their territory of Texas. The government hoped the Americans would build towns and help settle the land for them. Thousands of Americans came to Mexico. They liked the idea of a new land where they could find adventure and fortune.

By the 1830s, there were more Americans than Mexicans in Texas. Many American settlers did not pay taxes to the Mexican government. Others kept slaves even though Mexican law did not allow it.

The Mexican president was General Antonio Lopez de Santa Anna. He was a very powerful, strong leader. He refused to let the settlers ignore Mexico's rules. So, he announced that no more Americans could move to Texas.

This made the Americans in Texas very angry. In 1836, they declared that Texas was no longer part of Mexico. They called their new country the Republic of Texas.

The Texans hoped to become part of the United States right away. Sam Houston went to President Andrew Jackson to encourage him to **annex** Texas. But Jackson said no. He was afraid that Mexico would declare war on the United States.

The Lone Star Flag

The new Republic of Texas needed a flag. They designed one with a single star on it. This flag gave the territory a new nickname, the Lone Star Republic. Today it is the flag of the state of Texas.

Houston in Charge

A man named Sam Houston became the first president of the Republic of Texas. When the new nation formed an army, Houston was its commander in chief. He had fought in the War of 1812. Houston was an exciting man. He liked to fight and get into trouble. He became a legendary (LEJ-uhn-dair-ee) figure to Texans.

Sam Houston

Remember the Alamo

The Mexican leader, Santa Anna, would not let Texas leave Mexico easily. He led thousands of soldiers to Texas. The Mexican army surrounded a group of about 182 Texans in San Antonio at the Alamo.

The Texans refused to surrender. They held out for 12 days. Eventually they ran out of **ammunition**.

The Mexicans attacked the fort. They chased the Texans from room to room. The Texans fought hard with rifle butts, knives, and even their fists. But the Mexicans killed every single one of them.

This is the Alamo as it looks today. ▶

A little while later the Mexicans surrounded hundreds of Texans at a fort called Goliad (GO-lee-ad). Again, the Mexicans killed every single Texan.

The Texans trained hard. Meanwhile, the Mexicans got sloppy. They thought they had won the war already. On April 21, 1836, the Mexican soldiers were resting outside of the city of San Jacinto (SAN huh-SIN-tuh). Suddenly, Sam Houston and 900 Texans attacked them. In less than 20 minutes, the Texans captured or killed all of the Mexicans.

The Texans also captured Santa Anna trying to escape. They took him prisoner. He agreed to give Texas its independence in exchange for his life.

Inspirational Words

The Texans were very angry about the battles at the Alamo and Goliad. They thought the Mexicans should have taken prisoners, instead of killing everyone. The soldiers started saying, "Remember the Alamo!" to inspire each other.

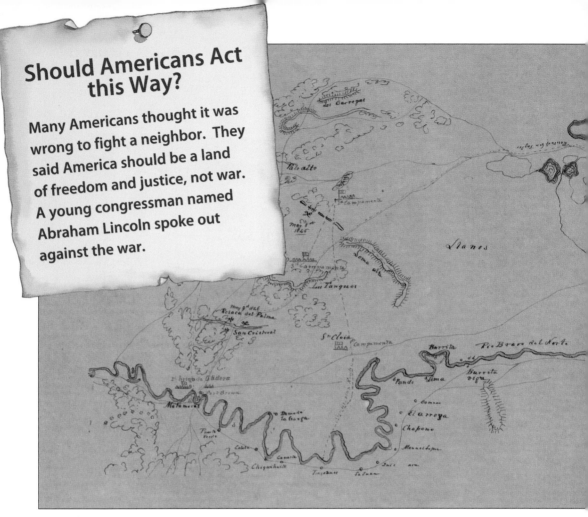

Should Americans Act this Way?

Many Americans thought it was wrong to fight a neighbor. They said America should be a land of freedom and justice, not war. A young congressman named Abraham Lincoln spoke out against the war.

▲ The Rio Grande Valley

At War with Mexico Again

After the war, the two sides disagreed about the border between Texas and Mexico. Mexicans thought Texas ended at the Nueces (nu-A-suhs) River. But, the Texans said they owned the land all the way to the Rio Grande (ree-O GRAN-dey). This border would make Texas twice as big.

In 1845, the United States prepared to make Texas the 28th state. President James Polk sent soldiers to the Texas border in case there was trouble. General Zachary Taylor led them. The soldiers moved into the area near the Rio Grande. The Americans considered this part of their country. The Mexicans thought it was theirs.

Mexican soldiers attacked and killed some Americans. President Polk went to Congress. He claimed that the Mexicans had killed soldiers "on American soil." This was not exactly true. But it worked. Congress voted to declare war on Mexico in May 1846.

Zachary Taylor

Old Rough and Ready

Zachary Taylor was a brave leader. Taylor was 62 years old when he went to Mexico. He wore an old, faded uniform and a big straw hat. His men loved him. They called him "Old Rough and Ready." Taylor became a famous war hero in Mexico. Later, he became the 12th president of the United States.

▲ **General Winfield Scott and his troops enter Mexico City.**

Heading South to Win the War

General Taylor and his men battled through northern Mexico for months. The Mexicans were brave fighters. But, they did not win any battles. Soon, the Americans held the capitals of three Mexican states.

At the beginning of 1847, President Polk decided to change strategies. He sent American soldiers south into Mexico. He wanted them to conquer Mexico City, the capital. He thought this was the only way to make Mexico give up.

General Winfield Scott was in charge of this new mission. The Americans kept hoping the Mexicans would surrender. But, Mexico refused to accept the Rio Grande as the border of Texas.

After many months, the Americans made it to the Mexican capital. Scott's army attacked Mexico City on September 13, 1847. They took the city by that night. The next day, a group of Mexican leaders surrendered to Scott.

It took many months to **negotiate** (nuh-GO-she-ate) a treaty. Finally, in February 1848 both sides signed the Treaty of Guadalupe Hidalgo (GWAH-duh-loo-pay ee-DAL-go). The Americans paid Mexico $15 million for their lands.

The Gadsden Purchase

American businessmen wanted to build a railroad line that would stretch across the continent. In 1853, a railroad specialist named James Gadsden (GADZ-duhn) went to Mexico. He asked if the United States could buy a large area across southern Arizona and New Mexico. It would be a good place to run the railroad line. Mexico was desperate for money. The government agreed to sell the land for $10 million.

The Last Frontier

By the 1860s it seemed like the United States had grown as much as it could. The country spread from ocean to ocean. But, one man kept working for a bigger America. William Seward was the secretary of state for Presidents Abraham Lincoln and Andrew Johnson. He was enthusiastic about helping America grow.

Russia had controlled Alaska since the 1700s. The land seemed to have little value. It was hard to use or to defend, since it was so far away from everything. Seward worked out a deal with the Russians. The United States would pay $7.2 million for Alaska. This worked out to about two cents an acre for an area twice as big as Texas.

▼ **Treasury warrant for the purchase of Alaska**

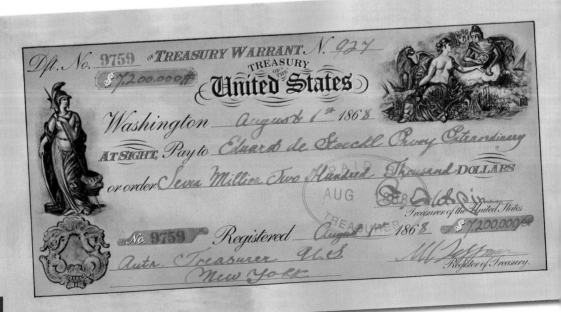

Many people made fun of Seward's plan. They thought Alaska was worthless. Some called the deal "Seward's Folly." Seward had to work very hard to get Congress to approve the deal. It passed the Senate by only one vote.

In 1898, gold was discovered in Alaska. The land also held other valuable resources like coal, copper, oil, and timber. Alaska turned out to be worth billions of dollars to the United States.

With the addition of Alaska, America had tripled its size in just less than 70 years. American settlers continued moving west. The once wild land provided opportunities for millions of people. The young United States was soon one of the richest nations in the world.

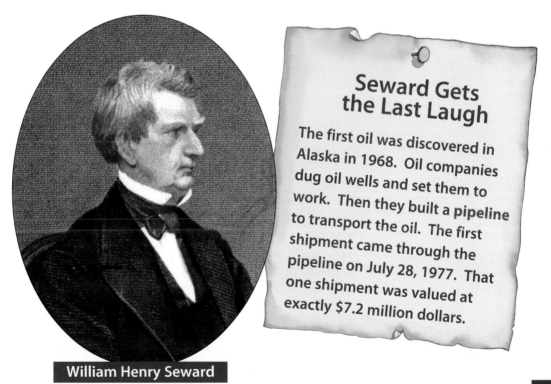

William Henry Seward

Seward Gets the Last Laugh

The first oil was discovered in Alaska in 1968. Oil companies dug oil wells and set them to work. Then they built a pipeline to transport the oil. The first shipment came through the pipeline on July 28, 1977. That one shipment was valued at exactly $7.2 million dollars.

Glossary

ammunition—supply of bullets and shells for guns or cannons

annex—to take a new piece of land and add it to a country that already exists

citizens—people who are loyal to a country and receive protection from it in return

dictator—a ruler who makes all decisions by himself and does not care what other people think

diplomats—people who represent their country's government to the governments of other nations

doctrine—a statement of government policy

expedition—a trip that people take with a particular goal in mind

legendary—something or someone that is very famous and stays well known for years

natural resources—things that humans need that come from the earth and the sea

negotiate—to discuss in order to work out an agreement on something

pipeline—a series of pipes used to move liquid from one place to another

territories—areas of land controlled by a country, but outside the borders of that country

treaty—agreement between countries to end a war